IMAGES
of England

MALDON
AND THE
DENGIE HUNDRED

The unique skyline of Maldon can be admired from the towpath of the Chelmer and Blackwater canal with, from left to right, the Congregational church on Market Hill with the British Schools building in its grounds, the tower of St Peter's church, Cromwell House, the top of the Moot Hall and the triangular spire of All Saints' church. Until 1873 the tall buildings in the centre of the picture were those of the Maldon Union or Poorhouse but by the time of this view, around 1910, they would have been furnished apartments, dwelling houses and a dame's school.

IMAGES
of England

MALDON
AND THE
DENGIE HUNDRED

Patrick Lacey

TEMPUS

A greetings postcard sent on 12 May 1910.

First published 2002
Copyright © Patrick Lacey, 2002

Tempus Publishing Limited
The Mill, Brimscombe Port,
Stroud, Gloucestershire, GL5 2QG

ISBN 0 7524 2487 4

Typesetting and origination by
Tempus Publishing Limited
Printed in Great Britain by
Midway Colour Print, Wiltshire

Contents

Acknowledgements

I must once again thank the Trustees of the Maldon District Museum for permission to consult their archives and to use material found there in the preparation of this book. The help of John Prime, co-ordinator of the Maldon Society photographic archive, was much appreciated. I also have reason to thank Len Barrell, Betty Chittenden, Ken Stubbings and George Ginn for their assistance. Without help from my wife, Pamela, the material would not have been kept in good order and the compilation could not have been so readily completed. I have used many images from my own postcard collection and thanks should be given to the unknown photographers of these views; elsewhere acknowledgement has been given whenever the name of a photographer is known. I have drawn on the collection of the late Dennis Swindale for the railway images. The Maldon District Museum will benefit from the proceeds of the sale of this further selection of local images that I hope will give great pleasure to all.

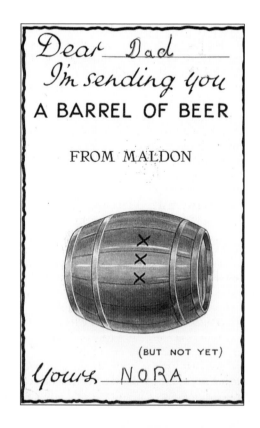

Dear Dad I'm sending you A BARREL OF BEER FROM MALDON (BUT NOT YET) *Yours* NORA

Introduction

It is generally agreed that the best book on the town of Maldon was that written by Edward Arthur Fitch in 1894. It appeared as a year book, which, in addition to containing tide tables and a list of tradesmen, gave much information on the town and surrounding countryside, together with a review of its early history.

In this work, *Maldon and the River Blackwater*, Fitch wrote that the borough had lost much of its dignity: its separate parliamentary representation had gone; its port authority had gone; its separate police force had gone; but it remained a healthy little town that had good sewerage and good lighting. Its pathways and roadways were well maintained and the water supply pure and sufficient. The struggles to achieve this satisfactory state of affairs have been chronicled in recent times by David Hughes in his excellent book, *The Maldonians*, which can be commended to all interested in the town

Maldon and the Dengie Hundred, a compilation of photographs, postcards and other printed matter, follows the area's history from the end of the Victorian era through the First World War to the inter-war years when Maldon was promoting itself as being ideal for holidays, health and beauty – 'the Pearl of East Coast Estuary Towns' – and then to the Second World War when so many of the local populace were involved in activities on the Home Front.

These years, between 1895 and 1945, are regarded as being the 'golden age of the postcard' and it is from postcards that over half of the images have been taken; the period 1900-1914 is particularly rich in material. At this time the postal service was so good that a young man visiting Maldon in 1908 could write a postcard to his parents in Ilford on a Saturday giving details of his expected arrival time home on the following day knowing that the card would get there. This could be regarded as almost the equal of today's text messaging!

The images on the postcards covered a wide range of subjects that included the latest news items. In the inter-war years the subjects of the postcards became more restricted with only the main tourist attractions in the vicinity being covered, but to compensate there was the appearance of 'snaps' from inexpensive cameras. Some of these have been included in this book where they give a sense of period. Some official photographs are also included together with printed ephemera.

Since my first book of images, *Maldon and Heybridge*, was published in 1996 there have been great developments locally. The District Museum that features items from the social history of the past 200 years has opened in the Promenade Park, and the Maldon Society has established a photographic archive, held on computer, that can be accessed at the Maeldune Centre in the High Street. Copies of old photographs can be obtained from the Centre at very reasonable cost. A similar scheme is in action in Burnham where the local museum is firmly established in its own premises on the waterfront that were once part of Tucker Brown's boatyard.

The Dengie Hundred, one of the ancient divisions of the county of Essex, may seem to be for the most part a vast desolate area with many acres of sparsely populated land reclaimed from the sea, but within in it there are interesting villages and one small town, Burnham-on-Crouch, that outstripped all the other communities in growth and gained classification as an urban district in 1898. During the fifty years covered by this book the population of many of the other settlements actually fell.

Maldon was regarded as the gateway to the Dengie for most of Queen Victoria's reign. Prior to the opening of the railway in 1889 from Wickford to Southminster through Burnham, with the branch to Maldon West, carriers provided a goods delivery service on a daily basis from Maldon to Burnham and Southminster and on three days a week to Tillingham and Bradwell-juxta-Mare. From 1848 a horse omnibus connected the two major centres of the Dengie peninsula with the railway at Maldon on four days each week.

The branch line from Maldon to Woodham Ferrers was not a success, closing to passengers in September 1939. Photographs of it are rare and it is pleasing to be able to include several from the late Dennis Swindale's collection that have never previously been published. The line from Wickford to Southminster was far more successful, giving the horticulturists and farmers of the Dengie easy access to the London markets and bringing a greatly increased number of visitors to the area, especially yachtsmen to Burnham. This line has survived into the twenty-first century.

Throughout the book, with the exception of some of the groups of workers at John Sadd & Sons, I have attempted to name those portrayed. Some of these names are missing and some will be incorrect. It would be splendid if any corrections or additions could be conveyed to the Maldon Museum to be recorded in the archives, thus making this volume truly interactive.

Partick Lacey
April 2002

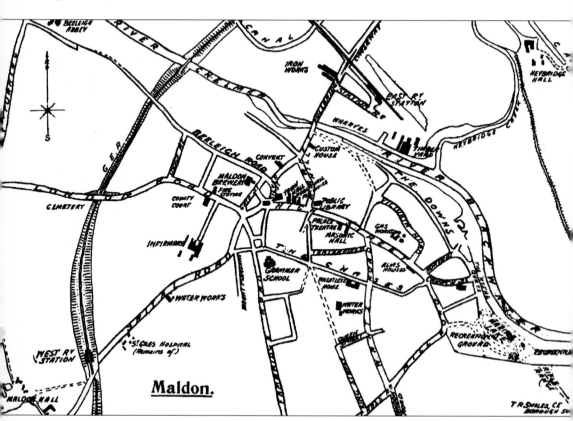

Map of the borough in 1907, drawn by the Borough Surveyor, T.R. Swales.

One
A Sense of Occasion

Towards the end of the First World War a Thanksgiving Week was held, with a gun emplacement being built by a detachment of troops in a shabby looking High Street. The gun had seen action at the battle of Cambrai. The ladies' and gents' hair dressing salons of Dibben and Sons can be seen on the right. The next shop seen is Samms, family grocer, and then Goodey, corn merchant and seedsman.

Edward Arthur Fitch – wearing the mayoral robes and regalia of Maldon – with Fanny, his wife, and their son, christened Thomas Maldon, were photographed in 1888 on the occasion of the presentation of a silver cradle by the Corporation. Derek Maldon Fitch, son of Thomas, is president of the Maldon District Museum Association, and in 2001 he donated the cradle to the Museum where it is displayed.

The home of Dr Henry Reynolds Brown, No. 70 High Street, is shown decorated for the coronation of George V in 1911. On that day the doctor was hospitalized in London suffering from scarlet fever. There had been an epidemic and he was Medical Superintendent at the Isolation Hospital. Happily he made a good recovery and continued to serve the Borough as Medical Officer of Health and as a family doctor into the 1930s. This fine house was demolished around 1933 and Woolworth's Bazaar was built on the site, which is now occupied by W.H. Smith.

Members of G Company, 5th Essex Regiment prepare to line the High Street on the occasion of the coronation of George V on 22 June 1911. The photographer has chosen a rather unfortunate moment to record the scene and it is to be hoped that the troops were 'standing easy' at the time and not attempting a less than successful drill movement!

11

All Saints' church as it appeared in the late 1920s, with a gathering of elderly gentlemen by the war memorial, which was erected in 1921. On the left is the water trough inscribed, 'To a good mother who lived and died in this town 1864-1900'. Recent research by the Maldon Archaeological Group has identified the mother as Mrs Lucy Hicks, and discovered that the dates are those of her residence in the town rather those of her life span.

The Mayor and Mayoress, Alderman and Mrs Laver Clarke, appear in this official photograph of 1929 with the Recorder, Charles Jones; the Town Clerk, F.H. Bright; Aldermen Turner, Baker and Furlong; the councillors, including one lady, Miss Ada Freeman; and the borough officials.

The Moot Hall as it appeared in 1938. The ARP (Air-Raid Precautions) poster should be noted – concern about the possibility of air attacks was growing.

The fleet of vehicles belonging to the Maldon Fire Brigade is lined up outside the original fire station in London Road before appearing in the 1937 Carnival. The newly acquired pneumatic-tyred appliance leads the way, followed by its solid-tyred predecessor and, lastly, the hand-pumper of 1877, which is now safely housed in the Maldon Museum.

The Rose Queen and her attendants with the Mayor and Mayoress, Alderman Laver Clarke and Mrs Clarke, are seen on the balcony of the Moot Hall during the 1935 Carnival. Margaret Hutley was the Queen with Marjorie Carr, Kathleen Mitchell, Edna Taylor and Betty Thorogood her attendants. Amongst others on the balcony are Jimmy and Mrs Gozzett, Walter Thorogood and Mr Morley.

A photograph by Cyril Osborn portrays the Rose Queen and her most elegant attendants in the garden of Albert Bunting's house, No. High Street. The original picture bears on the reverse the signature of Robertson Hare, star of *Rookery Nook*, the visiting celebrity at the Carnival.

The Rose Queen also had an entourage of 'Rose Petals', pictured here on Albert Bunting's lawn. They are thought to be, from left to right, back row: Beryl Joselyn, Doreen Pyman, Brenda Saville, Barbara Tebbell, Joy White, Margaret Hutley (Queen), Monica White, Olive Humphries, Margaret Balls, Florence Dudeney. Middle row: Mary Balls, Zoe Thorogood, Pam Clark, Daphne Pinyoun, Beryl Firman, Mary Playle, Joy Playle. Front row: Nancy Keeble, Liz Barnard, Doreen Tebbell (sitting), Ann Baxter, Mary Nicholls.

Fred Spalding photographed twelve mayors, town clerks and mace bearers of Essex inside the old Chelmsford Corn Exchange. They were attending a thanksgiving service at Chelmsford Cathedral to celebrate the twenty-first anniversary of the Diocese held on 31 October 1935. Maldon was represented by the Mayor, Alderman A.L. Clarke, the Town Clerk, C.H. Cloughton, and the Mace Bearer, J. Waldock, each seated fifth from the right in their allotted rows. The Maldon mace, dating from the reign of James I, is the largest on show, as befits the second oldest town in Essex!

A military detachment, led by the Town Band, marches past the Ship and Anchor at the lower end of the High Street. Medals are worn and there appears to be a group of veterans at the rear. The date is unknown, but could this be connected with the opening of the Avenue of Remembrance on the Promenade?

Two
Maldon for Health and Beauty

Hopefully the lady and gentleman, resting in their deckchairs, were in some way connected with the gaggle of children shown posing by the Marine Lake in this card sent from Maldon in 1925.

A well-laden, chauffeur-driven motor turns from Mill Lane into the Marine Parade some time around 1900. The Marine Lake has yet to be enclosed and the Promenade Lodge, to house the Park Superintendent, has yet to be built.

The more usual way to arrive at the Marine Parade would have been on foot or by horse-drawn vehicle. In this animated scene an important summer event is underway on the river and on the recreation ground, together with all the fun of the fair.

Dress styles may have changed over the passing years but people's behaviour remains remarkably constant. In this postcard posted in 1908 a booted and aproned girl pushes her younger sister to view a heavily laden sailing barge, proceeding up to Maldon for unloading.

Around 1910 all members of a family would have been well covered and in their best attire for an outing to the Marine Lake. A floating platform, with a small diving board attached, adds to the enjoyment of those allowed to swim.

Although encumbered by long coats, these young ladies are not prevented from messing about in boats. The extension to the Parade has been completed which dates this card to the late 1920s.

Unemployment was a problem for Maldon in the years that followed the First World War. One way in which it was tackled was by obtaining government grants for public works rather than by giving benefit. In September 1924 thirty-five local men were employed in such a scheme, widening and extending the Marine Parade. On 21 June 1925 the Mayor, A.L. Clarke, officially opened the extension that was to prove a popular attraction, as can be seen in this postcard sent in 1932.

Cyril Fox from Streatham took these three photographs on a visit to Maldon in 1920. They show the fishing smack, *MN14*, resting by the Bath wall whilst junior Maldonians paddle in the river. Below, there are two boatmen awaiting customers to hire their day-boat and a larger sailing vessel, full of passengers, heading away from Maldon on a day trip towards Osea.

A visually arresting image of the late 1930s was the introduction of modesty-protecting changing shelters on the shingled foreshore of the river.

By the late 1930s seaside dress for adults and children became far more casual but there are plenty of sensible but stylish hats in evidence.

Between the wars just outside the Promenade Lodge, now the Maldon District Museum, there was to be found this 14lb gun, a relic from the First World War. Participants on a Bermondsey Sunday school outing to Maldon in the early 1930s are using it as a climbing frame. The girl in front is Elizabeth Daniels, whose own grand-daughter now lives locally. The building with the small spire was St Mary's parish room.

The successful water polo team of the Maldon & Heybridge Swimming Club are seen in 1921, having won the Essex Cup. Matches were played on Sunday afternoons in the Marine Lake and attracted sizeable crowds, especially when the Plaistow Swimming Club opposed Maldon. Herbert Brewer holds the inscribed ball and William Andrews the cup.

On 1 January 1935 the Eastern National Omnibus Company bought out the network of local services run by J.W. Gozzett as Quest Motors, and replaced them with their own services. Later they constructed a large garage and bus station in the High Street from which they ran special excursions and tours, particularly during the summer months.

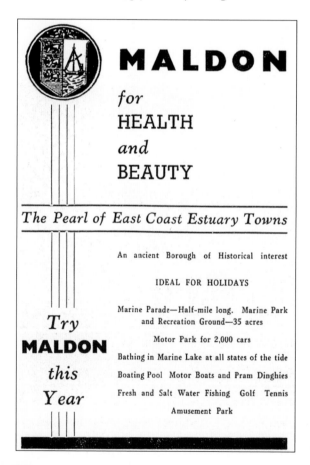

MALDON

for
HEALTH
and
BEAUTY

The Pearl of East Coast Estuary Towns

An ancient Borough of Historical interest

IDEAL FOR HOLIDAYS

Marine Parade—Half-mile long. Marine Park and Recreation Ground—35 acres

Motor Park for 2,000 cars

Bathing in Marine Lake at all states of the tide

Boating Pool Motor Boats and Pram Dinghies

Fresh and Salt Water Fishing Golf Tennis

Amusement Park

Try **MALDON** *this* Year

From *Maldon & District Official Guide 1938.*

24

Three
Commerce and Industry

From the Downs footpath there is an excellent view of the industrial heart of the town looking very fresh and neat in this photograph from the end of the nineteenth century. Maldon Ironworks is on the far left and, next door, the roller mills of E.T Baker and of Samuel Garratt.

Some of the oldest houses in the town are to be found at the top of the High Street. The first shop on the left belonged to the Tew brothers, Edward and Arthur, who had taken over the bakery business started in 1867 by their father, Robert. Their sisters, Mary and Harriet, ran a millinery outlet from the same premises. On the right is a business, run by Fred Seymour Moore, that bears the sign 'ye olde shoppe for tobacco, snuff and cigars'.

This row of shops, Nos 27-33 High Street, was demolished in 1917 to reveal a view of All Saints' church after a long campaign conducted in the local press. At the time of this postcard view, around 1908, Victor Brock, confectioner, Spurgeon & Son, Maldon Permanent Building Society, Luigi Volta, refreshments and confectionery, and Oxley Arthur French, fishmonger, poulterer and game dealer, occupied the shops respectively.

This High Street scene, appearing in Poole's *Book of Views of Maldon*, was taken before the 'great fire' of 17 January 1892. It shows the shop on the corner with Market Hill belonging to W. Archer, milliner, that he had occupied from 1889. The shop was unscathed by the fire but those of his neighbours, James Fuller, boot and shoemaker, and Edward Rudkin, hairdresser, were so seriously affected that they had to be demolished.

Bunting's have been butchers with commercial premises in the High Street for well over a hundred years. In the 1920s their immaculate delivery van extended their family butchery service throughout the district.

Museum visitors will be familiar with this picture as Tesco presented a giant version of it to the museum in 1998. After the 1892 fire the shops between the Moot Hall and Market Hill corner were soon rebuilt with the exception of the gap in the building line that was to be filled by the new GPO in 1907. The bearded gentleman standing in the shop doorway is Richard Poole, the proprietor. He published the postcard from which this image is taken and also compiled the *Book of Views* already mentioned.

This mock Tudor building at No. 51 High Street, that was the General Post Office from 1907 until 1980, now houses Dorothy Perkins, the ladies' outfitters. Earlier Ortewell & Son, ironmongers, occupied this site and it was here that the fire broke out in 1892 reducing this shop and all its stock to rubble. A swinging copper kettle, Ortewell's trade sign, marks the building to which that firm moved after the fire.

Edwardian ladies scurry by the cycle shop of L.S. Hicks where machines are available for hire. The adjacent shop, a corn and seed merchant's, also belongs to the Hicks family. Beyond this is yet another cycle agent, John Beale, and even the Swan Inn, next door, is advertising accommodation for cyclists. The craze was at its height! The appearance of the Swan will not be familiar as the frontage was fashionably altered around 1908 but fortunately much of the original fourteenth-century structure remains within.

The building on the far left was for many years a doctor's residence. Later it became a high-class boarding house that was purchased in 1933 by the County Council to become a children's home, known as The Gables. On the right is one of the elegant gaslights that continued to light the town until the early 1970s. In the centre the canopy of the Hippodrome can be seen extending out over the pavement.

Sheep were depicted in an oil panting of the 1880s by the artist, Keeley Halswelle, which has recently been returned to the town after an absence and can now be enjoyed in the reception lounge of the Blue Boar Hotel. It was this painting which lead to Robert Nightingale, a local artist, being commissioned to paint a similar scene except that a sunny day was requested as it was felt that the rainy scene was not good for the burgeoning tourist trade.

A herd of cows, either being driven to be milked or to new grazing, or perhaps to a field belonging to one of the butchers who had a slaughterhouse nearby. This was a common sight in the High Street around 1900.

Pigs were a less usual feature and far more difficult to handle in traffic. A herd of porkers are being driven from Mr Ratcliff's farm at Beeleigh to the East station as they were going for bacon. Alf Twitchett is behind them with Wallace Binder to the side on the pavement just passing Knightbridge, the tobacconists, and a willing lad is in front of them.

After the First World War farming became increasingly mechanised and the demand for tractors to replace the trusty horse grew. These Fordson tractors, seen outside Bates' Motor Works in Spital Road, are destined to fulfil this need.

The coal distribution yard belonging to the Maldon & Heybridge Co-operative Society, *c.* 1920. This is an unusual subject for a postcard. The yard lay behind the shops, owned by the Society, on the south side of the High Street. Houses and flats, belonging to a housing association, now stand on the site of the yard.

Opposite top: Some of the fleet of Austin and Morris cars, belonging to the Maldon Car Hire and Taxi firm, are posed for a publicity photograph in the car park just within the gates of the Promenade Park. On the far right the Promenade Lodge can be seen amongst the trees; it was then the home of the park keeper and is now Maldon District Museum. In the centre of the picture Volta's Café and Tea Gardens in Mill Road are advertised.

Bottom: On an afternoon in the late 1930s the wedding limousine, supplied by Maldon Car Hire that was owned by Joe Dykes, has transported a newly wed couple to their reception at the Swan Hotel in the High Street, watched by some interested spectators.

In 1925 the Southend Water Company promoted the first major water supply scheme in the area by excavating a huge reservoir at Langford to provide a supply of water to Southend abstracted from the Rivers Chelmer and Blackwater. A large main was laid from which some of the parishes of the Maldon Rural District could also obtain supplies. This photograph by Hazletine Frost depicts some of the army of workmen employed on the project and one of the steam cranes that they used.

Opposite top: This aerial photograph, taken in the inter-war period, shows the works of John Sadd & Sons surrounding the site of Maldon East railway station and its goods yard. To the right of the furthest siding can be seen the railway pond which was planned by the Eastern Counties Railway to be a dock for continental traffic being dug at the time of the construction of the station in 1848. The dock was never completed and it passed into Sadd's ownership, who had their hardwood-seasoning yard situated on its banks.

Bottom: In 1896 John Granger Sadd (1828–1900), patriarch of the family firm, had his photograph taken accompanied by some of his employees in one of the timber sheds. He is sitting in the second row, holding a bent cane walking stick, with his eldest son, John Price Sadd (1863–1929) on his right and Harry William Sadd (1866–1921), a younger son, on his left. It is interesting to note that even the youngest of apprentices were allowed to appear, sitting cross-legged in the front row.

From the 1870s John Sadd & Sons had used traction engines to shift great baulks of timber to their sawmills on the Causeway in Maldon. These were not universally popular. In 1871 Revd Thomas Knox of Runwell wrote to the *Essex Herald* to record that in the past week six of these ponderous machines had passed his house pulling huge loads of timber and remarking that 'It is bad enough to meet them in daylight but when they travel at night (as Mr Sadd's did last Friday) they are ten times more formidable to encounter! The noise, the smell, the steam and the glaring fire are enough to frighten any horse!' The machine and trailer are outside the magnificent railway station at Maldon.

The mammoth load has reached the timber yard on its trailer that had been constructed by Sadd's. Some of the men are identified, from left to right: John Raymond (?), H.W. Sadd (leaning against the trunk), Tom Flack, Joe Wisbey and Jack Panifer on the engine which had been on hire from Kirby of Maldon. Goods trucks are to be seen on the rail tracks behind the trailer. Sadd's had fought and lost an expensive legal battle with the Great Eastern Railway over access to the wharf side in the 1850s.

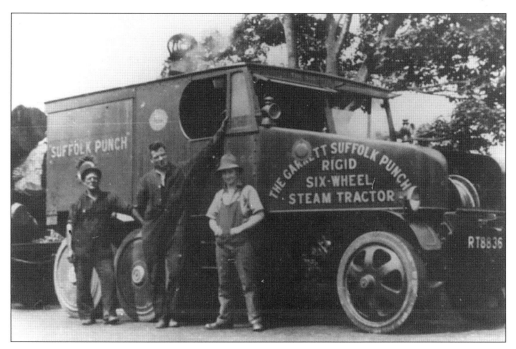

Another monster vehicle used by Sadds for shifting felled timber to their sawmills in Maldon was this Garrett rigid six-wheel steam tractor, built in Suffolk. The crew are Bob Atherton, Bill Woods and, in the hat, Tagel Sadd. A journey from Bury St Edmunds to Maldon with a load of timber took two days on the road.

On arrival at their site of work, around 1930, at a speed not exceeding 12mph, the driver of Sadd's Foden steam traction unit, Bob Atherton, and his mates, Arthur Vince and Cecil Murton, take a reviving mug of tea before commencing the heavy work of loading the trailer.

After the First World War lorries became an increasingly familiar feature on local roads. John Sadd & Sons owned several Ford trucks and articulated vehicles. In 1933 they purchased their first diesel-engined Foden and, later, a petrol-engined Bedford articulated lorry. It is seen here in 1937, unloading using the impressive gantry system built at the timber yard. This system can be seen in the aerial view on page 35.

The unloading gang, aboard a vessel moored at Sadd's wharf, appear in this picture from 1937. They were responsible for carrying lengths of timber, balanced on their heads, up the angled gangplanks, shown to the left, from the holds of barges and coasters to the stacks, seen in the background.

The gaff cutter yacht *Ripple*, which belonged to the Sadd family, is under way on the River Blackwater. She was designed and built by John Howard in his Maldon boatyard in 1877 and continued to sail until the 1950s.

On a long, warm Edwardian summer's day the family is aboard *Ripple*, cruising in local waters. A professional skipper was employed and for many years this was 'Daddy' Hedgecock.

This beautiful vessel, *Thoma II*, was designed and built by John Howard at his Maldon yard in 1909 for Mr Frank Callingham of Great Baddow. The barge yacht was 100ft long overall and, as shown here, dwarfs the working sailing barge, belonging to Rutt and Gutteridge, which lies ahead of her on Fullbridge wharf. With a skipper and a crew of three, *Thoma II* cruised far afield from the River Blackwater and ended her days as a motor yacht in the Mediterranean.

A remarkable early photograph (before 1875) of the handsome five-storey building that was Beeleigh Mill. It contained twelve pairs of millstones driven by the force of the River Chelmer that was maintained to give a 13ft drop in water levels. Another five pairs of stones were driven by the power of steam provided by a Wentworth beam engine installed in 1845. The house to the right is Beeleigh Falls House, built in 1858, which in 1875 was occupied by the mill owner, Henry Ward, and his family.

On 12 March 1875 the mill was destroyed in a terrible fire that could not be brought under control, despite the efforts of the manual pump of the Borough fire brigade aided by the fire engine of the Essex & Suffolk Insurance Company. The mill was never rebuilt and in this early amateur photograph the remaining walls and the tall chimney shaft, all that had been left standing, can be seen. The surviving three-arched bridge, beneath which lighters could pass to be loaded and unloaded, is also well illustrated.

The fire had destroyed the watermill but, fortunately, the engine house and the steam-driven engine within were saved. The Essex Water Company, who made the building safe and thus secured the survival of this valuable piece of industrial archaeology, eventually purchased the site. It is now managed by Essex County Council and Maldon Archaeological and History Group, which hold open days each September. This postcard from the 1930s shows the ruins of the mill.

The fine bill-head of the Raleigh Roller Mills when it belonged to Samuel Garrett. It was shortly afterwards to pass into the ownership of William Green.

This smart lorry is being loaded at Green's roller mill at the Fullbridge with Fred Gorham at the front of the vehicle and ? Radley and Ernest Ward in the open door on the right at first floor level. In the lorry supervising the loading is Harry Green.

One well-known business in the inter-war years was the Maldon Poultry and Fruit Farm in Fambridge Road, whose proprietor was Alderman Harold Granger. He became a very successful competitor in fruit-growing shows, winning outright the coveted gold vase for the best dessert apple in the Empire at the Imperial show in three successive years.

The apple harvest in 1937 was an excellent one. The fruit has been carefully picked and placed into boxes ready for packing. Mr Granger and his staff were assisted by three young ladies, recently qualified horticulturalists, who lived in a converted railway carriage on the farm.

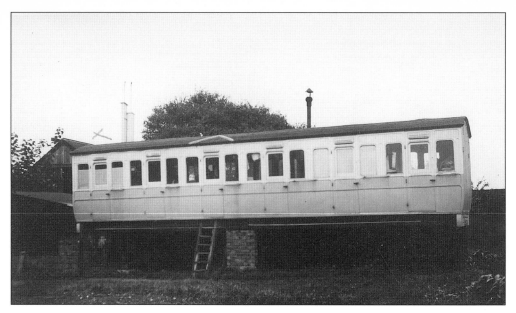

Miss M.E. Loveridge, one of the helpers, has marked with a cross the section of the carriage at the fruit farm which served as her bathroom. She recalls that picking, grading and packing apples were her main jobs although plums and cherries were also grown.

Harold Granger seen in 1938, the year in which he died at the age of sixty-nine. He appears a very contented man standing on the edge of the Blackwater estuary contemplating the view of his small sailing vessel, *Emma*, safely at anchor. His name lives on with Granger Avenue, together with Orchard Road and Close, occupying the land where his business once thrived.

Four

Education and Entertainment

This postcard, sent in 1904, depicts London Road with, on the left, the building that was used as the boarding house for pupils attending Maldon Grammar School. Behind this was a shed-like construction that served as the schoolroom. This proved inadequate for an increasing school roll and a new school in Fambridge Road duly replaced it.

The Chairman of the County Education Committee officially opened the building in 1907. It was designed by Mr P.M. Beaumont, a local architect, and Fred Spalding photographed it when it was brand new. Initially the school taught pupil-teachers of both sexes but admitted only boys as pupils. Girls were first admitted as pupils in 1919.

The 1919/20 season must have been an epic one for the members of the Grammar School football team, which was under the supervision of Mr Montague Williams. The end-of-season photograph showed that, although four caps for footballing merit had been awarded, the team had been reduced to ten men, one carrying an arm injury!

A heat at the Grammar School sports day at a time when men were men and hurdles really were genuine hurdles. The winner of this race was Leavett with Cocks in second place.

Some of the fastest young ladies competing at the Grammar School annual sports day in the 1920s provide an exciting finish to the 100-yard race. Lanes, carefully marked out with tape, separate the runners with V. Baldwin, the winner, hitting the finishing tape ahead of I. Saunders in second place.

Children of All Saints' Church of England Junior Schools combine to celebrate May Day with a maypole erected in their playground. The windows of houses in London Road can be seen opposite.

In 1927 a group of local lasses perform maypole dancing in the grounds of the William Wheatley Home for Orphans in America Street, where the present day District Council Offices are situated. The young lady nearest to the camera, looking at the photographer, is Myrtle Sargent; clockwise from her are Gwen Wisbey, Ada Mitchell, -?-, Elsie Pitt, Joyce Mead, -?-, Winnie Bloomfield, Violet Chapman, ? Livermore, ? Willsher, Min Braybrook, ? Jocham, Joyce Lynn, -?-, -?-, -?-, -?-, -?-, Edna Rayner, -?-, Kath Simmons, Phyllis Askew, -?-.

A classroom scene at the Council School in Wantz Road around 1930 shows that the children sat in orderly pairs at double desks and had recently completed a study of the Holy Land with a goodly number of palm trees and camels in evidence.

These are some of the Grammar School girls of the 1920s photographed by Hazeltine Frost. It is not known who they were or what they were supposed to be when they appeared at a school concert, except for the fact that one young lady was called Edna!

The combined choirs of Maldon schools are seen occupying the stage at the Public Hall. The hall was erected in the High Street in 1860. An audience of 600 could be accommodated. During the late nineteenth century it was in use as a corn exchange as well as for general entertainment. From 1922 it became the All Saints' Parish Hall and remained so until sold in 1964. It then served as a sorting office for the GPO.

HIPPODROME
MALDON

Re-opened after extensive alterations by the Mayor, Councillor
J. W. TANNER, on Thursday, December 22nd, 1927.

Resident Manager: T. W. SMITH   **'Phone: 168**

THE HIPPODROME

PRICES OF ADMISSION (including Tax):—

1/6 : 1/3 : 9D. : 6D.

(Seats at 1/6 may be booked in advance without additional charge).

**TIMES: Monday to Friday. Continuous from 7 p.m.—10.30 p.m.
Saturdays at 6 & 8.15 p.m.**

Matinees on Wednesdays, Saturdays & Bank Holidays at 2.30 p.m.

The Hippodrome Picture Palace opened in the High Street in 1909. Seating was provided for an audience of 450 with stage facilities that included two dressing rooms. It was designed primarily for silent moving pictures with a programme of films that was changed twice weekly, but dramatic entertainments and variety shows were also advertised. It was modernised in 1927 for 'talkies' with a special opening performance on 22 December of *The Better 'Ole* which starred Syd Chaplin as 'Old Bill'. The most obvious external sign of the renovations was the greatly enlarged canopy extending over the pavement. The cinema closed in March 1936 and was turned into shops.

A magnificent house, The Trees, stood in the High Street until 1935 when it was demolished to make way for the King George's Place development that included a fine cinema, the Embassy. Its interior was luxurious with carefully chosen colour schemes, the most up-to-date ventilation and heating system and the latest projection equipment. There was seating for 1,250 patrons with no seat being directly behind another. A café was provided within the building, serving anything from a cup of tea to a hot meal. The Embassy Court retirement flats now occupy this site.

To complete the delight of a trip to the movies a mighty Wurlitzer organ was installed that was played by Leslie James when the Embassy first opened in March 1936. He was succeeded by Cecil (Vic) Hammett, seen here in 1946. Vic had been touring in Europe when war was declared and was interned in Germany spending most of the war years there. On his return he married Ivy, an usherette at the Embassy.

The decorated cart entry from the Maldon & Heybridge Co-operative Society for the celebration of the coronation of King George V in June 1911 was impressive. Labour is portrayed shaking hands with Capital on a veritable mountain of CWS goodies.

Summer entertainers were a feature of the Marine Parade. In 1905 Messrs Cross and Williams provided the show with their Royal Bohemians. Their acts must have included a ventriloquist, in addition to many musical numbers, some of which must have involved twirling the sunshades seen in front of the stage.

By 1934 the entertainers had become more polished. They were known as Uncle Sam's Maldon Minstrels and are shown in their alternative costumes. From study of autographs signed for an enthusiastic fan they included Uncle Sam, Uncle Harry, Auntie Edie, Frank Dee and Billy Magee!

James Matthams opened the Dolphin Inn at No. 102 High Street as an alehouse in 1847. It finally closed its doors in 1907 with the last licensee being Henry Conn, whose name appears on the sign. The inn had a chequered history as in 1888 the landlord lost his licence for harbouring ladies of the oldest profession on his premises. After closure the building was divided into two shops.

Two of the town's now closed hostelries are shown on this postcard. The White Lion, on the left, existed from the late eighteenth century until 1910. The producers of Shrimp Brand ales owned it and also had a store close by on the Fullbridge Wharf. On the right is the Ship Hotel, which survived until 1961 before being converted into flats.

From 1823 until 1964 the Duke of Wellington, an inn belonging to Gray's brewery, stood on the corner of London Road and Wellington Road, the last landlord being Mr Keogh. Subsequently the pub was demolished and All Saints' Parish Hall was built on the site.

In this 1912 view of Silver Street the Blue Boar Hotel announces that it has stables and a motor garage with inspection pit. A metal notice to the left of the carriage entrance advertises Bentall Motors (All British) that were being built less than two miles away in Heybridge. A second notice gives details of trips in the *Annie* to Osea Island. A little further down the street is the Bell Inn, which was a licensed house from 1848 until 1958, the last landlord being Harry Pepper.

The Star in Wants Road, that opened its doors as a public house in 1848, survived until 1978. The brewers, Carrington, Nichol & Co., had an agency store to the rear of this building.

A public house demolished in more recent times was the Chequers, a very ancient inn with written evidence for its existence dating back to 1624. Ken Stubbings in his history of Maldon inns points out that the name 'Chequers' indicates a place where money, tokens or goods are exchanged. It is therefore ironic that a newly built branch of Barclays Bank should have replaced this pub in 1987. Are the men on the left awaiting opening time?

The Railway Bell, situated just outside the gates of Maldon East station, was a conversion of a house that had occupied a site on Potman Marsh long before the arrival of the railway in 1848. Taking advantage of its position, its owner, Charles Ridley of Chelmsford, then converted it into an inn that survived until the 1950s.

The Temperance Hotel and Coffee House was situated on Market Hill next door to the Congregational church; indeed, a board on its side wall gives the time of services. In 1907 the proprietor was Charles Simons, who was also caretaker at the church. Permission was obtained in 1963 to change its use to offices; these were used by the probation service and as an annexe for the Essex County library service staff.

Five

The Streets
of Maldon

The Prince of Wales public house, that survived until 1910, is seen on the left of this view of Market Hill. Three years later it was described in a Directory as being a Temperance Hotel under the charge of Joseph Chandler, and in recent times it was the Cromwell Guest House. Until 1873 the large building had been the Union workhouse but by 1910 it had become apartments for letting with one section housing a dame's school. Could some of the pupils of the school be depicted here?

The first business premises of the local Co-operative Society, that had its origins amongst the labour force at the Iron Works in 1873, was this building at No. 44 Market Hill. The Society flourished and soon moved to a larger site further up the hill. When this view was taken around 1910 the shop was occupied by William Flack's drapery business.

Traffic hazards of the late 1920s are in evidence with mounted troops, a sports car and a juggernaut from a petrol company competing for road space. An added problem is the railway company van that is most dangerously parked. The buildings on the left, Nos 22 and 24 Market Hill, were pulled down in the 1930s and a small public garden now occupies the area.

By 1910 residential development had taken place along the north side of Cross Road, which included these houses that are today Nos 60-72. In 1913 the second house from the left was the manse occupied by Revd Henry Parrott, minister of the Primitive Methodist church in Wantz Road. The lane opening beside it was then regarded as an extension of Queen's Avenue but subsequently it became known as Manse Chase.

Lodge Lane is shown gated and with a substantial brick wall dividing it from the adjacent Dykes Chase in this 1905 view. The lane led to an elegant building, erected in 1807, that was part of the six-acre barracks site occupied by troops ready to repel a threatened Napoleonic invasion. By the beginning of the twentieth century these substantial houses had been built along the right-hand side of the lane.

West Square is seen as it appeared between 1895 and 1945. Doe Motors latterly owned the buildings in the centre and redeveloped them in the mid 1950s into a modern garage facility. In this view it is the furniture shop of John and George Burnes. The small house on the right belonged to Joseph Payne, who ran a coach-building business behind it.

The image of an efficiently managed town is presented in this charming picture of Spital Road with attractive street lighting, good pavements and a well-groomed surface to the unmade road. This scene from the early 1900s pre-dates the development of both Cherry Gardens and Highlands Drive.

This postcard shows Mizpah, the Home of Rest, in Wantz Road, founded by Miss Henrietta Sadd as a charity enabling poor women from London to have a refreshing break in the country. In 1912 a resident sent this view to her daughter saying that she felt homesick. 'There is not much to see here, only fields, hedges and lanes. There is a picture palace but it does not open until 8 p.m. by which time we have to be in!'

Miss Sadd provided another home for such women at The Rest, a building adjacent to her own home, Hill House, on Market Hill. The women are to be seen strolling and resting in the Hill House garden, enjoying their recuperative holiday.

The Carpenters Arms in Gate Street was the outlet or tap for a brewery that occupied an extensive site stretching between London Road and Beeleigh Road. Gray's owned the brewery from 1865 until 1954, when it closed. Edward and Sarah Mead were landlords at the Carpenters from 1875 until 1903.

These buildings, long demolished, stood on the site of the present-day No. 136 Wantz Road and were occupied at the beginning of the twentieth century by Herbert Blowers, who was a beer retailer and furniture dealer. Earlier, he had also run a pork butchery here. It is difficult to see how all these activities were divided between the two shops.

From the distant past until the 1920s a smithy and wheelwright's workshop stood at the end of Mill Road at its junction with Wantz Road. In 1913 the blacksmith working from these premises was William Burch with Thomas Marsh, wheelwright. Two bungalows belonging the Price Almshouse charity have replaced these buildings.

Foundry Terrace was built by Joseph Warren for his workers in 1865, close to the ironworks on the Causeway where they were employed. Four of the dwellings had six rooms and eight had four. The terrace was demolished in the late 1960s, having been used, latterly, as temporary housing by the Borough Council.

With the exception of a marked off cricket pitch, cows graze on the fields that are now occupied by the Plume School. The first houses in Fambridge Road and, behind them, the buildings and houses in Mount Pleasant can be distinguished. The array of chimneys on the Union Workhouse, later to become St Peter's Hospital, can also be admired.

In 1927 Henry and Florence Brown moved from Ilford and purchased a large plot of land in Spital Road where Henry built a family home, No. 63. He also built the first houses in Acacia Drive, then an unmade road, which can be seen in the background of this family group taken in his garden in 1930. Henry and Florence are in the back row with their son-in-law, Leslie Clark and their daughters, Mabel, Violet and Dorothy, are in front of them with the grand children, Ruth and Michael.

Six

Heybridge, The Basin and Mill Beach

The Chelmer and Blackwater Navigation was constructed in 1797 to enable goods to be conveyed between Chelmsford, the county town of Essex, and the Blackwater estuary. A horse-drawn barge has just worked through Beeleigh lock in this view taken from a postcard, sent in September 1908, and is on its way towards Heybridge.

A hut, dating from 1918, was moved from Osea Island and re-erected in Goldhangar Road, Heybridge. It became a general stores and tea room where Mrs O.J. Clark was licensed to sell tobacco and postage stamps. However, more popular than these must have been Mill Beach rock, which figures largely in advertisements both on the building and in the shop window in this view from around 1936.

The canal was fourteen miles long with eleven locks. A group of children are seen playing on the canal towpath close to the Wave bridge in Heybridge.

The Radio Stores of J.W. Collear at Heybridge served a most important function in the supply of valves and batteries for the wireless sets that were appearing in many homes in the 1930s. Above everything else, the task of recharging of accumulators to power the sets was performed here.

In the 1930s The Towers, the largest private house in Heybridge, became a convalescent home run by the Ancient Order of the Good Shepherd. Later, during the Second World War it was used as a prisoner-of-war camp and in the post-war era the Borough Council used it for temporary housing purposes.

Edward Hammond Bentall, the iron founder and by far the largest employer in Heybridge, built the Towers in 1873 as his own home. He made pioneering use of reinforced concrete in its construction in the form of blocks cast on site. The large elegant mansion was built to the design of Charles Pertwee, surveyor and architect of Chelmsford, but it incorporated many of Bentall's own ideas, including a heating system of ducted hot air with strategically placed vents. It cost the very considerable sum of £65,000. The house was set in beautifully landscaped

gardens complete with a large lake with swans and an impressive cylindrical shaped avairy set amongst fir trees. A high wall also made of concrete blocks surrounded the whole estate of ten acres. It was here that a combined Sunday schools' outing came, around 1910, to enjoy the extensive grounds. The names of the many participants have not been recorded; it would be most interesting to learn who they all were. The house remained as the home of the Bentall family through three generations until being sold in the 1930s.

The children of members of the Maldon & Heybridge Co-operative Society are celebrating Childrens' Day, *c.* 1910. By the 1930s the local society organized a large annual flower show to which all 'co-operators' were invited.

The Heybridge Band that was associated with the British Legion provided popular musical entertainment at such events.

A magnificent Heybridge wedding – but who are the people in this very special photograph? The hats and bouquets are marvellous, the best rug has been brought out for the small bridesmaids to sit on and even the family canary has a place in this record of a beautiful day. The setting is amongst the terraced cottages, built in 1875 for workers at Bentall's factory, so it is certain that at least one, if not more, of the men would have been employed there.

By 1931 the Isolation Hospital for the Maldon area, situated in Broad Street Green, had obtained an ambulance in the form of a Model T Ford. The driver is Arthur Hume and the young girl is his daughter who became Mrs Trowles of Staplers Heath in Great Totham.

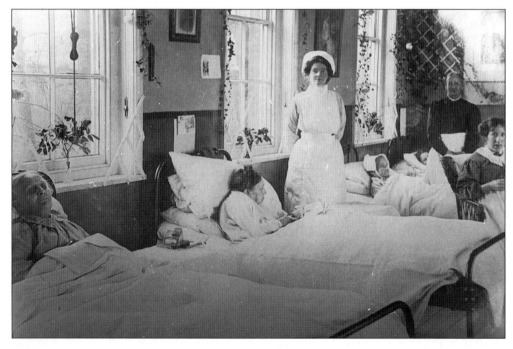

Frank Reynolds, who was working in Maldon as a professional photographer, took this picture of the women's ward in the Isolation Hospital in Broad Street Green in the 1920s.

A horse-drawn barge heads towards Heybridge Basin, passing the home of Mrs Putt. There is a landing stage at the end of her garden, which has been marked X on this postcard sent in September 1913. The writer remarks that the house was very damp and cold in winter! The large building on the right is the magnificent warehouse belonging to Bentall's.

The Navigation met the River Blackwater at a specially constructed sea lock that was just over 100 feet in length and capable of admitting vessels of 300 tons displacement. A community of watermen, seafarers and canal-related workers grew up at Heybridge Basin. In this postcard sent in 1926 a Thames sailing barge is moored just above the lock.

This small community required licensed premises and the Old Ship, formerly known as the Chelmer Brig, was actually owned by the canal company. The milk delivery cart seen in the background on Lock Hill provided non-alcoholic drinks! As demonstrated, the balance beams of the sea lock provided a very convenient resting place for the senior basiners, from where advice could be dispensed to all using the lock.

The Basin was also served by a general stores and post office that appeared on this postcard sent in 1932. This shows that the stores had a very smart delivery van of which they were proud.

Canal barges are shown lying in the river outside the Basin. They were being used for the trans-shipment of timber from large vessels anchored in deep water at Colliers Reach and then this cargo was either unloaded at the basin or conveyed, via the canal, fourteen miles inland to the timber yards in Chelmsford.

A business that was successful during the recession of the 1920s and '30s was ship-breaking. The firm of May and Butcher performed this just off the seawall beyond Heybridge Basin where they also had a wood yard and a large saw mill.

The Mill Beach Hotel became licensed premises in 1894 with William Chambers as the first landlord. Benjamin Handley took over the establishment in 1904 when it was advertised as a prime tourist attraction with good fishing and boating available. An ornamental lake was constructed where rowing and, presumably, sailing could be practised regardless of the state of the tide.

According to an early *Official Guide to Maldon* the Mill Beach and its surrounding area was developed as an 'Ideal Riverside Holiday Resort', situated just two miles from the town. In early days it was promised that every train would be met but by 1938 the Guide suggested to intending visitors that they made use of a convenient bus service.

These bathing belles are taking advantage of a lengthy landing stage that at high tide gave easy access from the Hotel to the river for swimming or for embarkation onto visiting pleasure craft.

The ladies of the Maldon Swimming Club are portrayed in relaxed mood at Mill Beach with time for a break in training, a snap for the album and, in the case of two young ladies, a quick ciggie. This photograph is from the album of Lily Keeble, later Joslin, who was Maldon's champion lady swimmer of the 1920s.

The river is over a mile wide at this point and there is safe bathing from the pebble beach. On this postcard, sent in June 1939, Frank writes to Norm in Birmingham to say that he is having a fine time with perfect weather, warm sea and plenty of girls: perhaps the bathing beauties of the previous pictures!

By 1938 comfortable, well-equipped bungalows with gas lighting and cookers were available as holiday accommodation at Mill Beach. Alternatively bell tents erected on the surrounding meadowland could be hired. Towing caravans were attracted to the area just before the Second World War and, increasingly, in the immediate post-war years when they became a firmly established feature.

Seven

By Steam Train to the Dengie

In the early 1930s J.E. Kite photographed this train of two six-wheeled carriages and a luggage van travelling between Maldon and Woodham Ferrers. The locomotive was a class G4 0-4-4 tank engine, No. 8105, which was withdrawn from service in 1938.

The Maldon West line was closed to passengers on 10 September 1939 but continued to have a daily goods train from Woodham Ferrers until 1953. The track to Maldon East was retained for a further six years and this enabled a railway enthusiast special to be run in April 1957 that was the very last train to bring passengers to the station. The locomotive was No. 68628, an 0-6-0 tank engine of J67 class. The tunnel entrance can be seen beyond the train with its further end opening into the goods yard that is now the West industrial estate. Because of it situation in a deep cutting and its early closure, photographs of this station are rare and this one by Herbert Springett is much valued.

Opposite, top: A busy scene at Maldon East is captured in LNER days with No. 7643, a J15 0-6-0 tender engine, about to leave on a train for Witham. The signal is cleared for the line ahead but the driver has yet to board. In the bay platform is No. 7574, a class F4 2-4-2 tank engine, on the branch train to Woodham Ferrers via Cold Norton.

Bottom: One long-gone piece of Maldon that may have special significance for some is the Lovers Lane footbridge that enabled walkers, on the footpath to Beeleigh, to cross the railway line safely. Now one takes one's chance when crossing the Maldon bypass at this point. The track was removed in 1960 and the footbridge demolished in 1965.

The Great Eastern Railway opened a halt at Baron's Lane, Purleigh, on 10 July 1922. One employee, who could accept goods for onward transit but not deliver any items received, staffed it. There was no shelter for intending passengers; the building seen behind the porter's bicycle is a weigh house and store. Percy Philby is the railwayman with Sid Gatward, in the coalman's apron, by his side.

Sid Gatward ran the coal delivery business from the railway yard at Baron's Lane. He is pictured in the 1930s loading his dray from a coal wagon in a siding. At a later date these sidings were used to store old carriages made redundant by electrification schemes elsewhere on the LNER railway system.

Cold Norton was the only intermediate station between Maldon West and Woodham Ferrers when the line was opened in October 1889. The platform signs read 'Cold Norton for Purleigh and Stow Maries' but later, when both of these places were served by halts, the signs were altered to read 'Cold Norton for Latchingdon'. This station had an excellent water supply and this was taken advantage of by the local farmers, who would send a horse and cart with some churns to be filled when their own supply was low.

Something of a rush hour is taking place at the well-kept and imposing station at Cold Norton with three members of the staff and six passengers awaiting the arrival of the train for Maldon West and, then, East. Sadly the entire station site has now disappeared under the houses and gardens of Green Trees Avenue.

This is the only known photograph of the very basic unstaffed halt at Stow St Mary, taken in the summer of 1939 by S. Neaves. The incumbent of the neighbouring church had insisted on this version of the name for the halt when it opened in 1928. The Halt did not survive long and was closed together with the other stations between Woodham Ferrers and Maldon East in September 1939. The area of the station is now a nature reserve.

This could have been the train for which the passengers at Stow St Mary and at Cold Norton were waiting. The locomotive is No. 8302, an F7 2-4-2 tank engine photographed leaving Woodham Ferrers with a train for Maldon. This particular locomotive was withdrawn from service in 1931 and is seen here towards the end of its useful life.

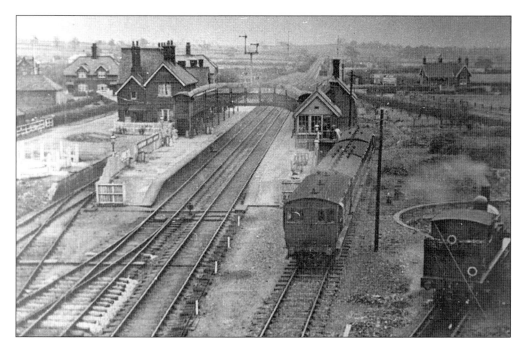

Woodham Ferrers was a junction station with the line to Maldon going straight ahead and the line to Southminster curving to the right. The Maldon line was always lightly used and became the subsidiary route. From 1890 until 1894 an express ran from Southend to Colchester, via Maldon West, using the triangular junctions at Wickford, Maldon and Witham.

The Great Eastern Railway always favoured the spelling 'Woodham Ferris' for this station. A class M15 2-4-2T is being given the right of way in this view from around 1910. This particular locomotive, No. 671, was withdrawn from service in 1913.

North Fambridge was provided with a railway station in 1889 that had a full range of buildings, a handsome footbridge and a passing loop. A train is approaching from Burnham but both the stationmaster and the porter appear more interested in the photographer's activities.

Althorne was a more modest station, being situated in an unpopulated area on the edge of the marshes but it had the reputation for being well managed and was a frequent winner of best-kept station awards.

Burnham-on-Crouch station was a larger establishment, as befits a town. A class N7 0-6-2 tank engine, No. 69616, is shown about to depart for Southminster in the very last days of steam operation in 1956.

The terminus at Southminster in LNER days, with the appearance of a model railway. The branch line engine, No. 7171, a class F4 2-4-2T, is being replenished at the coal stage, a short distance from the engine shed, while its carriages rest in the platform.

The railway to Southminster opened up this thinly populated area of Essex to the London markets, encouraging the development of smallholdings and giving a boost to local agriculture. A cattle market was held each Tuesday in Southminster and the lime-washed cattle trucks can be seen on the cattle loading bay platform.

This map was printed on a postcard produced around 1910 by the Bacon Geographical Establishment and sent from Maldon to an address in Christchurch, New Zealand.

Eight

The Dengie and Osea Island

St James is the parish church of Dengie, one of the least populated villages of the peninsula and Hundred to which the village gave its name. Parts of the church may date from the twelfth century but it was extensively rebuilt in the fourteenth century, using yellow bricks imported from the Low Countries in addition to Roman bricks obtained from the fort of Orthona at Bradwell.

The Hurdlemakers' Arms, Woodham Mortimer, is featured on this postcard posted in 1908. George and John Taylor ran a hurdle-making business in nearby Hazeleigh in the 1920s.

An interesting postcard that shows the relationship between St Nicholas's church, Hazeleigh, and Hazeleigh Hall, an ancient moated manor house, home of the Alleyne family. During the demolition of the church in 1922 a piece of plaster was found bearing the Commonwealth arms, which had replaced the royal arms during Cromwell's rule after the Civil War. Alas techniques were not then sufficiently advanced for this to be preserved for posterity.

Cock Clarks is a substantial hamlet, which is administratively attached to Purleigh. It had its own pub, the Fox and Hounds, and village hall. This shop acted as a post office in addition to being a grocers and drapers. At this time there was a Methodist chapel and there had been a school until 1915.

The corner of Chimney Lane and Birchwood Road, which leads to Purleigh, is seen here. The chimney referred to is one that was situated in a brick and tile works at the far end of the lane.

This beautiful picture, published as a postcard, was sent in 1926 with the expressed hope that the recipient would like the new surroundings of the sender. A groom pauses outside the premises of D.T. Brown, grocer and baker, at the foot of Church Hill. The single-storey staff accommodation for the rectory can be seen on the right at the top of the hill.

Young heifers, sharing space with free-range poultry, are evidence of the mixed farming practised at Purleigh Hall Farm. In this view All Saints' church tower is in the centre of the picture and, on the left, there are the farm cottages of the Hall. Beside them is the building that was once a wheelwright's shop and forge.

96

The centre of Purleigh, seen around 1900. The Bell Inn, then having served as a hostelry for around 300 years, is on the right and the village store is on the left. Between the buildings are the great barn and the cart shed of Purleigh Hall.

This most satisfying building housed a grocer's and draper's business from the mid-eighteenth century until the early 1970s. The village post office was situated here with a telegraph facility installed in 1902, initially underwritten by the Parish Council. Sarah Olney ran the business between 1905 and 1920.

Until the end of the nineteenth century Cold Norton consisted of a number of dwellings straggling along the road to Latchingdon but in 1889 the railway arrived, as seen on page 87, and a station and goods yard were provided, with a Railway Inn built close by.

This large building, Norton Hall, and its associated farm belonged to the Foyle family of bookshop fame. The church of St Stephen, Cold Norton, that stands adjacent to the hall, was completely rebuilt in 1855, and possessed a bell tower, seen through the leafless tree, which unfortunately became unsafe and had to be removed.

Stow Maries is one of the smaller parishes of the Maldon District with a population of 176 in 1891. The rectory is a very fine building that accompanies an interesting fifteenth-century church dedicated to St Mary.

George Graylin's grocer's and draper's shop at Stow Maries is shown at a time when the local clergyman was trying to have the village renamed Stow St Mary. He had succeeded with the railway company (see page 88) and here is evidence that he had success elsewhere as the shop bears a post office notice headed 'Stow St Mary'. The doors of the shop were closed for the final time in January 1972.

These cottages, nestling behind a surrounding embankment, appear in imminent danger of inundation in this high-tide view from the sea wall at North Fambridge. In the course of the terrible East Coast floods of 1953 they were flooded to bedroom height but they continue to survive to the present day.

Burnell's stores and post office at North Fambridge are depicted on this 'between wars' card. A rack of postcards for sale can be seen just within the open shop doorway.

An early form of transport serving North Fambridge was the ferry, which since time immemorial had carried goods, passengers and animals across the River Crouch to South Fambridge. It continued to do so until just after the Second World War.

Controversy reigned in the late 1970s when permission was granted for St Michael's church, Latchingdon, to be converted to a house. E.A. Fitch, writing in 1894, pointed out that this church, over a mile from the village, had not been used for forty years, except as a mortuary chapel. The tower had fallen and the chancel had also gone, leaving only the nave and south porch as pictured here.

The Street in Latchingdon, around 1900, was lined with timber-framed, weather-boarded dwellings. The small building between the houses was the local post office but, when this was moved to a nearby shop, it became a branch of the County Library.

A team of local builders and decorators pause from their labours for photographic purposes. They are working on one of the houses that made up the lengthy row of cottages, known as the Terrace, situated in the Street.

An extremely attractive lady is portrayed around 1910 outside a house in Latchingdon, known as the Granary. She is Kathleen Clear, who, on marriage, became Mrs Ansell.

On a fine summer's day between the wars the Bugg family are harvesting on their farm, known as Ulehams, in Latchingdon, This farm, of over 200 acres, is situated between the lower Burnham road and Bridgemarsh Creek, and is crossed by the railway line to Southminster. Around 1900 it had its own wharf that was visited by sailing barges, bringing manure and feed stuffs to the farm and taking produce away.

An earlier harvest scene is recorded in this photograph of Barnes Farm in the neighbouring parish of Althorne.

The arrival of the railway opened up Althorne for the development of villas, particularly on the hilly ridge, that gave extensive views over the River Crouch. The writer of this postcard says that it was her father that had built the house but she, having now moved away, missed the convenience of the railway station and the fine roads.

Creeksea (or Cricksea) is a small hamlet in the parish of Burnham. In 1861 there were thirty-eight dwellings here and a resident population of 175 souls. A church, an alehouse, called the Leathern Bottle, and a schoolroom existed.

A trip to the river's edge in the 1920s was a pleasant outing. There were the Elizabethan Tea Rooms for sustenance and views over the River Crouch to be enjoyed.

The importance of Creeksea was that, for centuries, it was the embarkation point for the ferry across the Crouch to Wallasea Island and, thence, into the Rochford Hundred. The rights of ferriage belonged to the Cricksea Ferry Farm on Wallasea, where the Cricksea Ferry Inn was also to be found.

Burnham outstripped the other villages of the Dengie peninsula in development and in 1898 was designated an Urban District. With the arrival of the railway it became a popular centre for yachting and the Royal Corinthian Yacht Club opened a clubhouse in 1893. It was followed in subsequent years by other yachting and sailing clubs.

A photograph by W. Barker of Queen's Road, Burnham, shows a congregation meeting in the open air in the early days of the twentieth century. The pianist's hat should be noted on top of the instrument. From which church or chapel these good people came is not known. There were many nonconformist and revivalist organisations in the Dengie Hundred at this time including the Marsh Mission at Coleward Farm and the Peculiar People's chapel at Tillingham.

A ferry across the River Crouch, the third to be mentioned in this book, is seen taking aboard passengers for Wallasea at the quay in Burnham in 1936. This ferry survives and is particularly active during the summer months.

A mile north of the town of Burnham, next to a farm, stands St Mary's church. The juxtaposition of this ancient building, dating from the fourteenth century, with the flock of sheep, makes this image an appropriate one as great flocks of sheep were raised on the nearby marshes. Large cheeses were made from the ewes' milk and Burnham flourished as the port that dealt with this commodity.

Southminster was the principal village of the Dengie Hundred with a weekly market. At the beginning of the twentieth century a police station and courtroom were built adding to its importance. The windmill, seen on the right, lost part of its sails in a gale in 1912 but continued in production powered by a steam engine. It was finally demolished in 1929.

Life in Southminster around 1910 is brought to a halt by a visit from a photographer. A group of local workers that includes a telegraph boy and postman then pose rather stiffly outside St Leonard's church. The church's appearance was more satisfactory at that time with its tower, dating from the fourteenth century, still intact.

Tillingham is one of the larger villages in the Maldon District with a population of 951 in 1891 falling to 683 by 1951. This view down South Street shows the Congregational chapel on the left.

The church school of St Nicholas had a school roll of 135 in 1905 when the headmaster was W.A. Chell. Some ten years later it was resolved at a meeting of the Guardians of Maldon Union to buy twenty pairs of clogs for children of the marsh districts. Clogs would be stronger and warmer than boots and not so tiring when walking the two or three miles to school!

Tillingham is a most attractive village with many timber-framed cottages around its central green or Square. It is seen here in a photograph by Fred Spalding, *c.* 1910. Directly opposite is the General Stores and, to the right, the cycle repair shop of J. Kemp.

A new market cart for a client from Asheldam is proudly presented for photographic record.

A splendid terrace of weather-boarded cottages and a shop, known as Cadge Row, is situated opposite the village school in Bradwell on the road to St Peter's chapel. The small building in the middle of the picture is the village lock-up.

The writer of this postcard considered Bradwell-on-Sea to be the prettiest village in the Home Counties. The decline in the importance of waterborne freight had been mirrored in the fall of population here from 905 in 1891 to 680 in 1951.

Many dwellings in the Dengie Hundred were picturesque but seriously lacking in amenities. This is Curds Cottage at Bradwell-on-Sea.

Bradwell Lodge was the rectory and home in the 1780s of the fearsome Revd Henry Bate-Dudley and, in more recent years, of Tom Driberg, MP for Maldon. Bate-Dudley funded many stylish alterations to this building to the design of the architect John Johnson.

The Maldon River opposite the Stone is wide and deep and provides a suitable anchorage for large vessels in times of recession. During the 1930s many proud ships lay here as shown in this view. The general store operated by the Stone Yacht Club is on the left. Cockles and shrimps for sale and deck chairs for hire are advertised on the right of this picture.

In the 1920s the Stone, or Ramsey Island as it had been known, was popular as a tourist spot for a day by the river on Wick Farm beach. A wick, in ancient times, was a dairy farm often situated on marshy ground where sheep were raised for their milk as much as their wool.

The temperance movement correctly regarded Frederick Charrington as being the 'white sheep' of the brewing family to which he belonged. In 1903 he purchased Osea Island, at agricultural prices, to establish a seaside health resort dedicated to the treatment of alcoholism. His grand plans, involving avenues of trees, many nursing homes and bungalows, did not come to fruition and the original 300-acre farm, has continued in production to the present day.

He also purchased a small twin–screw steamboat, *Annie*, that had previously worked on the River Irwell at Manchester. It was planned that this vessel should make trips twice daily from Maldon to the pier erected on the river frontage. She became a very popular addition to the tourist scene carrying day-trippers to Osea for picnics and bathing, in addition to making longer sea trips and occasional moonlight outings.

This view from Osea Island shows the full extent of the pier at the time of Charrington's ownership. The *Annie* has just arrived and another group of day-trippers will, shortly, begin to disembark. To the left are the seal pools designed to house some of these delightful animals, which occur naturally in the Maldon River, but here will be confined for the entertainment of the residents and island visitors.

A village store was established in the centre of the island, opposite the old farmhouse, to supply the needs of the inhabitants and those of visiting yachtsmen except, of course, that no liquor could be sold!

In 1904 Mr Charrington advised intending clients that 'besides the wild sea birds found on the Island, acclimatisation of foreign animals and birds will be carried out'. Three kangaroos were already on the island. Emus and cockatoos would be introduced, and seals would inhabit a small marine lake. Bearing in mind the nature of his clients' problems all this could be regarded as a high-risk strategy!

Horses are taken to water in the Osea pond in a scene reminiscent of a 'Western' rather than a spot only 40 miles from Mile End in east London where Mr Charrington had established his Great Assembly Hall and Mission. There was a natural supply of water but with the development of the island an artesian well was sunk to supplement it. From earliest times Osea had been part of the parish of Great Totham but, with considerable development promised, Maldon Borough wanted to take charge and levy rates!

In 1918 a base for the coastal motorboats of the Royal Navy was established on the island, which became HMS *Osea*, and housed a complement of up to 1,000 men. Ordinary Seaman Charles Jewell was one of the many sailors stationed here between June and December 1918.

The sailors were involved in the development, maintenance and repair of these vessels designed to carry either torpedoes, depth charges or to lay mines. The Navy retained the base until 1926. Many of the wooden huts were dismantled and then re-erected in Goldhangar Road and in Basin Road, Heybridge as dwellings or as, on page 70, commercial premises.

Steeple, with a population of 460 in 1891, falling to 330 by 1951, must have been one of the smallest places to have its own souvenir postcard. This card depicts St Laurence's church, extensively rebuilt by Fred Chancellor in 1884, the riverside at Steeple Stone and two views of the Street.

St Mary's church at Mundon was declared redundant in 1974, the centre of the village being at some distance from it. The parish was transferred to the care of St Mary's Maldon and the Friends of Friendless Churches adopted the church building. The church is noted for its weather-boarded bell tower and its Jacobean north porch.

In happier times, around 1906, St Mary's Mundon had an impressive choir. The incumbent sitting in the centre of the front row is Revd Leopold Bruhl with his wife, Lavinia, on his right. The choirboy on the far left of the front row is Max Solly with Joe Moss next to him. Second from the left in the second row is Alec Solly with Mr A.H. Wilkins, fifth from the left, and Mr Thomas Solly, then a lay preacher, seventh from the left.

Nine
The Home Front

The group leaders of local first-aid parties parade outside the chapel at St Peter's Hospital in 1942. The man on the far right is Jack Newton, with Wilfred Berridge next to him.

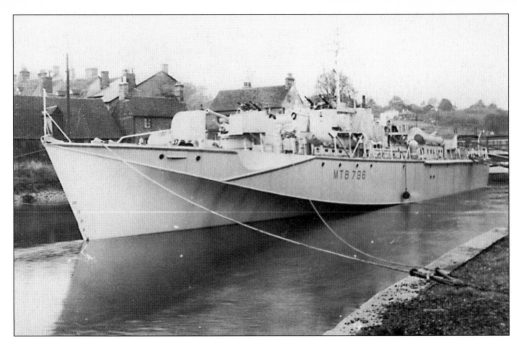

The completed Fairmile Type D motor torpedo boat, MTB 796, that had been built by Sadd's for the Royal Navy, is moored at Fullbridge opposite Sadd's wharf in early 1945. A fine model of this vessel, constructed for the boardroom by Aubrey Pettican, a craftsman at Sadd's, can be seen on display at the Maldon Museum.

Members of the staff of John Sadd & Son, who formed the construction crew of MTB 796 in 1944, are recorded in a photograph taken aboard the vessel. Aubrey Pettican, mentioned above, is on the far left of the back row.

Special constables and air-raid wardens are photographed outside the King's Head in Bradwell-on-Sea.

Bradwell-on-Sea air spotters of the Observer Corps, seen close to an observation platform. They are, from left to right, back row: Messrs Turpin, Scurrel, Dowsett, Murrells, Kemp, Mercier, Winter, Burch, Page. Middle row: Messrs Dowsett, Woods, Dowsett, Henrey, Chillingworth, Thorpe. Front row: Messrs Dodd, Argent, Beadell, Ballard, Birdsill, Burch. The identity of the gentleman in the trilby, on duty in the tower, is not known.

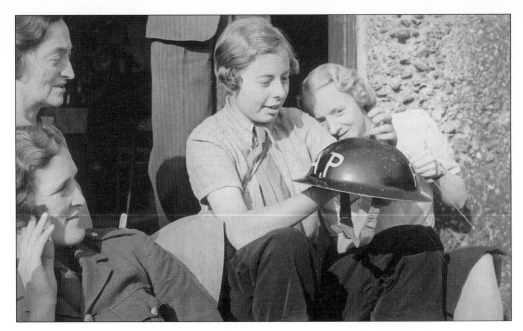

Members of the St Peter's Group first-aid party, inspecting recently received kit, are Mona Clarke, Olive Rawlinson and Dr Finlay, with Rena Burrell sitting in front of them.

The mobile first-aid post, acquired by the St Peter's first-aid group in 1942, is a most interesting conversion of a commercial vehicle for ambulance duties including blackout hoods on the headlights and white tips on the forward edge of the front mudguards. It is crewed by Olive Rawlinson, later Mrs Berridge, Mona Clark and Nurse Cooper.

A first-aid party is shown in action during a training session where they are handling a dummy victim. They are Percy Floyd, -?-, and Mr Pennick, working under the guidance of Tom Wright, the group leader.

The Heybridge first-aid party is portrayed with their smart vehicle bearing four stretchers on its roof. It had been designated as transport for sitting casualties and is painted to comply with blackout restrictions. The group leader is Cecil Vince with Eric Ward, Bob Lait and two others accompanying him.

An unknown member of the Auxiliary Fire Service stands outside a fire station well protected by sandbags. The old Borough fire station in London Road had been demolished in 1938 to make way for a much larger fire facility built behind it that has only recently been replaced.

The Maldon Home Guard photographed outside the Grammar School in 1945. Amongst their number in the back row on the right are Messrs Nichols and Edwards, in the middle row on the far left Mr Gladas and, fourth from the right, Mr Ball and in the front row, Mr Joslin in command.

The score card given to each member of the various civil defence teams at the end of the Second World War tells its own story of the efforts all had made in helping to protect the local area, comprising Maldon Borough, Burnham Urban District and Maldon Rural District.

This shows houses in Fambridge Road that were seriously damaged by a flying bomb on 25 September 1944.

CIVIL DEFENCE

Essex County—Eastern Area

(Maldon Borough, Burnham U.D., Maldon R.D.)

The following are the recorded figures for the European War, 1939—1945.

| Alerts | **1,174** |
| Incidents | **777** |

Bombs

High Explosive 1,628	Mines	83
Incendiary 24,844	Parachute Bombs	3
Phosphorous I.B. 39	Oil I.B.	43

Other Missiles

Flying Bomb V1 83   Rocket V2 54

Casualties

Killed 25   Injured 191

TOTAL MISSILES 26,778

T. J. HOWSON RUSSELL,
A.R.P. Sub-Controller,
A.R.P. Officer.

During the early years of the Second World War, when fuel supplies were low, W.J. Morrison, Chief Engineer of the Eastern National bus company, devised a wheeled gas-producer unit that could be towed behind the bus that it powered. All vehicles allocated to the Maldon depot were converted to run on gas.

The end of the war in Europe was celebrated on VE Day, 8 May 1945, with many street parties being organized. This particular one is in Maldon's Dagger Lane, North Street, where everybody seems to be having an extremely good time.